MINECRAFT DIARY OF A WIMPY ENDER DRAGON

Contents

One of a Kind

Hi there! My name's Ander but people like to cal

me Ender instead. I'm pretty famous and I am a

dragon and I live in the Minecraft Universe. My life

here is pretty unique compared to the other

inhabitants of Minecraft.

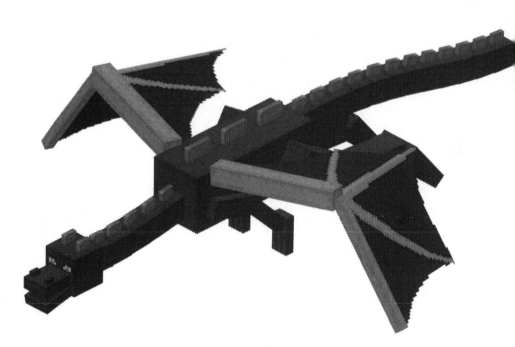

For one thing, I am a rather lonely dragon. Yes, while the place I live in is vast and big, it seems there are no dragons to be found. I was born and hatched into this world and have known no other.

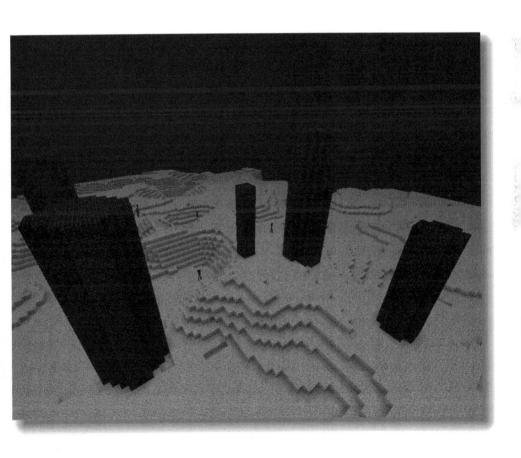

As a dragon living in Minecraft, I know that I am the only one of my kind. How? I am rather self-aware and being a curious little dragon, I took it upon myself to uncover this mystery.

t wasn't much of a mystery. Legends say there

were once 4 dragons, one for each realm; The

Overworld, the Astral World, the Nether and the

End.

Then when the players came, they had to prove their mettle, their strength or were simply looking for glory. One by one, they came and slaughtered the dragons.

Unfortunately, none of them survived long. The

Nether dragon, in a bid to protect himself tried to

cast some magic on him. The results weren't pretty.

He turned into a Wither and became a grotesque

version of a dragon.

He can still fly but he is nothing like me. Instead of

one head, he has three and no wings.

Moreover, he became a slave to his spell. He wanted immortality but in his haste, he must have mixed something up. Instead of immortality, he only comes alive when summoned in a certain manner.

Once he is summoned, he is so unused to the

freedom he gets that he destroys everything around

him and players will eventually destroy him after

summoning him. It is foolish and in many ways, a

little cruel of them but some only summon the

Wither for glory.

When it was my turn to get slaughtered, I opened

up a chasm and escaped into the End.

The End, Magic and Me

I think the only reason I managed to survive the scourge which killed my brethren is owing to the fact that I live in a place called the End and because of its unique nature.

The End is harder to reach for the players. Since I

am stronger at Magic, I was able to ensure that

finding the way here was harder as compared to

finding the way to the Nether.

Magic is also stronger here and I am more skilled at

it then the Nether Dragon would ever have been.

However, since I choose to seal myself in this place,

I have to say it was not always this pleasant.

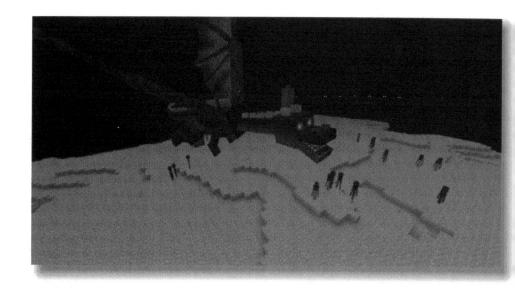

The End was a dark and gloomy place so I created the Endermen. They are my friends.

While they have multiplied over time and I do not know every one of them, I have a bunch of friends among them, with different names.

There's Meren, Heren, Helga and Togo and more but I get along with them best.

As Endermen, I didn't have much to draw inspiration from and they're all tall and black in color with purple eyes.

think this maybe the reason I get along well with

hem. I share the same coloring. I am also black and

ny eyes are purple in color too.

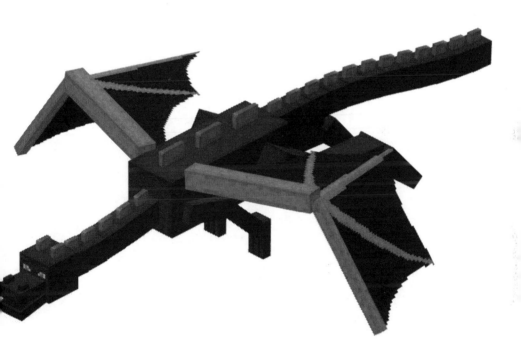

No one bothers to come here because of the Void.

The Void is a scary place to many but not to me. It is

a bottomless pit which surrounds the land around

me.

As I have the ability to fly, the Void does not pose any problems to me but I have seen what happens to anyone who falls in. They don't make it out alive.

Moreover, I live on Magic.

I have some magic crystals which the Endermen

helped mold into large rocks for me. These crystals

nourish me and when I am weakened, they help to

heal my wounds.

Like I said, I am more skilled at magic than others.

Disturbing News

One day, as I was lazing on the sands of the End, Heren and Meren came up to chat with me. They usually have information about the Overworld to share.

Since I do not set foot on the Overworld, my Endermen go and gather news for me. This is the best way I can ensure that no one catches sight of me and I stay updated with what is going on.

t is how I know most of my knowledge. At times

hough, I miss the Overworld but it is better this

vay.

One day, it will be safe to come to the Overworld and maybe, I can then begin to search for other dragons.

Heren and Meren did not have good news to share

with me today. They informed me that a player had

been overheard looking for the Ender portal. Heren

worried that he would find his way down to us but

t did not disturb me.

Many players try to find their way down to the End.

It is not always easy and usually takes them a lot of

time.

Often times, when the poor souls do make their

way down to see me, they are not prepared. This

fact amuses me to no end. I am a strong dragon and

in the protection of the End, I have grown large and

fearsome.

also do not need meat or fruit or vegetables. I can

ive off magic and my crystals have helped me grow

o this size.

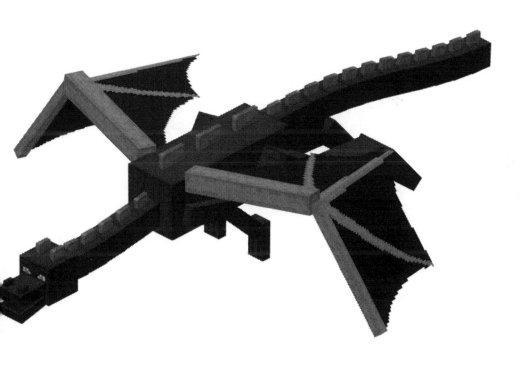

In the protection of the End, I have grown

thousands of years old and I am most probably, one

of the oldest things in Minecraft.

Sometimes, the players are so unprepared when they see me that they don't always know what to do.

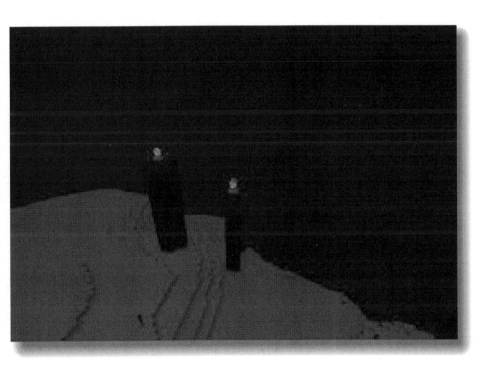

The first thing which many players see is my bright

purple eyes. Since the End itself is so dark, my eyes

appear like two amethysts in the sky.

While they are confused about it, I can often throw

hem down the Void or if not, at least deliver them

a major blow which hurts them.

The other Endermen also come to my aid. It is their duty to protect me.

I make sure that the poor player who wishes to slay me has to put up a good fight. No weakling can slay me with ease.

While Heren and Meren were worried about the player finding the way down to the End, I shushed hem quietly. I reassured them that I would be able o kill the player and we could resume our happy ife as it was.

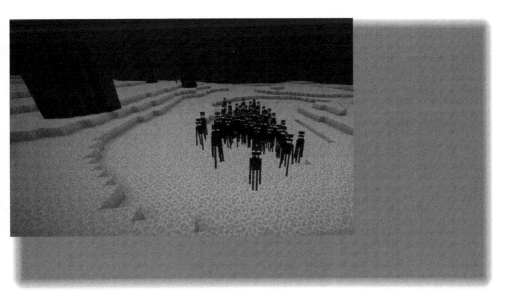

Calmed but not exactly reassured, Heren and Meren

did not bother me anymore and I close my eyes to

enjoy a luxurious nap on the sands.

The Player Approaches

t was two weeks after Heren and Meren had

nformed me that the player was searching for the

Ender portal when they told me that they had heard

hat the player had found what he was looking for.

Lazily, I brushed the sand off me and flew up to my

pedestal. If he had found the portal, it would not be

long before the player would be here.

needed to make it difficult for him to find me. Up

on my pedestal, I would be able to see him, long

before he saw me.

Heren and Meren informed the other Endermen about the intruder we were expecting now. We all waited in anticipation. I wondered if that player had made the portal ready or if he had only found it.

t did not matter though, I was used to sleeping on

my pedestal and I would not come down now until I

would be told that the player was gone or is no

more.

Eventually, I saw a bright light in the distance. The player had found his way to the End and he was holding his torch high to light his way. This made him a very easy target for me.

cast a spell on the Endermen, making them angry and frenzied and they began to swarm towards the player. If the player was not a strong one, he would soon die at the hands of the Endermen and I would not have to engage him in battle.

This also gave me a chance to see the kind of weapons he had. If he was impatient, he would have come here without the right equipment. On the other hand, if he knew what he was doing, his weapons would show it.

watched sharply as the player drew out a diamond sword. I hissed in anger. It appeared he was armored as well. This would be a difficult fight.

I watched as in the distance, he started to hack and slash his way through the mob of Endermen.

Few of them gave him wounds as well but he persisted, weakly and defiantly.

He continued to walk in my direction as he attacked the Endermen around him.

I knew that in a few miles more, he would be in the perfect position to attack so I watched his slow progress.

When he was only a few feet away from my pedestal, I let out an ear splitting roar. The player did seem surprised and stopped immediately.

While he watched, I swooped down quickly and gave him a blow on his head.

He Finds My Weakness

f he hadn't been wearing that diamond helmet, I

:ould have delivered him a fatal blow.

Jnfortunately, his helmet turned the fatal blow but

ie still got hurt a little.

I flew up, turned and then came at him again with

all my strength. This time, I struck him again but he

was ready too.

He slashed at me with his diamond sword. I flew away but as the sword cut into me, it did do some damage. Luckily, my magic crystals started to heal me immediately.

The magic I had allowed me to recover much faster from my wounds. I kept these crystals, particularly for moments like these and they were situated high on different pedestals.

As soon as the crystals started to heal me, they gave of small beams of light. The player drew out a cross bow and tried to attack me again. He shot all his arrows at me but I flew away, mostly unharmed.

took a few arrows but I healed as quickly as possible too. The player watched me curiously and then, suddenly, he started running.

I watched as I wondered what he was up to. Maybe

he had given up the fight. Suddenly, I felt sick to my

stomach. The player was trying to get up the

pedestals to the crystals.

Luckily, the pedestals where extremely huge but I

watched as the resourceful player pulled out a

ladder started to climb up. I wondered what he was

going to do next.

As I watched, the player pulled out his sword and started hacking at the crystal. I swooped and attacked him.

He had found my source of energy and he was damaging it. I knew if he succeeded in breaking the crystals, it would be the end for me.

I would not heal from any wounds I had taken and it he could then attack me freely. The player broke the crystal then turned to attack me again. I lunged at him and threw him to the ground.

He took some damage but it did not kill him. He looked puzzled but I grinned at him. One crystal was not my only source of energy. They crystals were separated, each on a tall pedestal of its own.

To destroy me, the player would have to go to each pedestal, destroy the crystal and then attack me. I watched as the player started to make for the other pedestal but was soon mobbed by other Endermen.

This was not going to be an easy fight for him but I watched as the stubborn player cut down the Endermen in front of him and moved on to the pedestal.

Here I attacked him again too but he took little

heed of me. He continued to hack and then broke

the crystal. Now I was really worried. There were

only two crystals left.

He broke both of them; it would be dangerous for me. Luckily, one of the pedestals was near the Void.

I hoped that the player would choose that one. If he went up to that pedestal, I could easily knock him into the Void and kill him.

I watched with bated breath as the player chose the

pedestal I was hoping he would. When he

clambered up, I swooped down at him. He was

ready and hacked at my tail with his sword.

nstead of flying in a wide circle though, I turned

around swiftly and pushed him with claws. The

player lost his balance and went tumbling down the

edge.

He not only fell from the pedestal though, he also fell down into the Void and vanished. The Endermen cheered and I was glad too but I was a little shaken.

This player knew my weakness and he was well prepared. If he had not wasted his arrows at me in the start, he could have beaten me easily. While the Endermen were ecstatically happy, I mulled over my problem.

For now, no solution came to mind. I simply asked them to repair my crystals and shivered in fear. I dread the day when one of the players manages to destroy my crystals.

It is a weakness which cannot cure. Yet, if I was to

truly master my magic skills, I would not have to

rely on my crystals.

I also send the Endermen to take other precautions.

I make them go up to the Overworld and dismantle

the Ender portal which has been found.

Armed with a little bit of magic, the Endermen can make it very hard for someone looking for the Ender portals.

For now, these precautions will have to do the job, I do not know what else to do. I feel that one day, I might have to either step out of the End to find out what to do next or maybe, I might just perish.

The Void may hold the answer to it all but as yet; I do not feel too threatened. I am a little scared of the Void itself so I shall not look for my answers there.

So I end this entry of my diary, scared and wimpy. I am a wimpy dragon but you must understand, I am the last of my kind and I have few friends.